"Do all the good you can, by all the means you can, in all the ways you can, in all the places you can, at all the times you can, to all the people you can, as long as ever you can." John Wesley 1703-1791

the bard from ballarat: International Edition

'a poet pursuing his passion for photographing this human experience'

thanks to everyone who had a part to play in putting this together
to the ballarat writers group and the greendale poetry group thank you for your feedback and support
a special thank you to the blue artz gallery in wendouree, who were the first to stock my work
thanks to the church retro cafe in ballarat, the first to request to stock my work, and host my launch
to all the other retailers and media outlets that have got behind me thank you
and to all those that inspired the poems or played a part in the photos thank you

Also available at http://nevillehiatt.com
Both these editions are printed on high quality glossy paper
Limited to 1,000 copies each with every copy individually hand numbered by the author
the bard from ballarat: volume 1
the bard from ballarat: volume 2

https://www.facebook.com/thebardfromballarat
https://twitter.com/thebardfromball

ISBN: 978-0-9923610-2-0

All poems and photographs by Neville Hiatt

'the greatest man'

from the greatest man you've ever known
and thoughts of how much you've grown
to staring at your pictures filling my suitcase of memories
from I love you forever
to I won't see you again ever
this suitcase is getting heavier
from blond to brown, thick to thin
the gaps in this suitcase are filling in
short to tall I've kissed them all
over the years one after another they all seem to fall
pictures, poems and cards all but markers in time
bra's, boots, panties, and hose
2 garter belts, who's they were God only knows
so many thoughts fill my head
yet I lay alone in my queen sized bed
memento's marking chapters of my life
I'd happily give up this suitcase
for just one introduction to my wife

'hugs'

leaving on the greyhound bus
amongst a lot of tears and fuss
I wish I wasn't leaving
sure would be a lot less grieving
sitting in bay no 3
gazing out the window at the fall colours on the tree
so wish I could stay
this I fervently pray
but as the door sounds to a close
another tear slides down my nose
as we pull away, I once again pray
that I could stay, even if just for one more day
but this is not the case
I am to be vacant once more from your sweet embrace
onward I must head
but tonight there will be tears in my bed
thank you for a wonderful stay
I hope to feel you once more some day

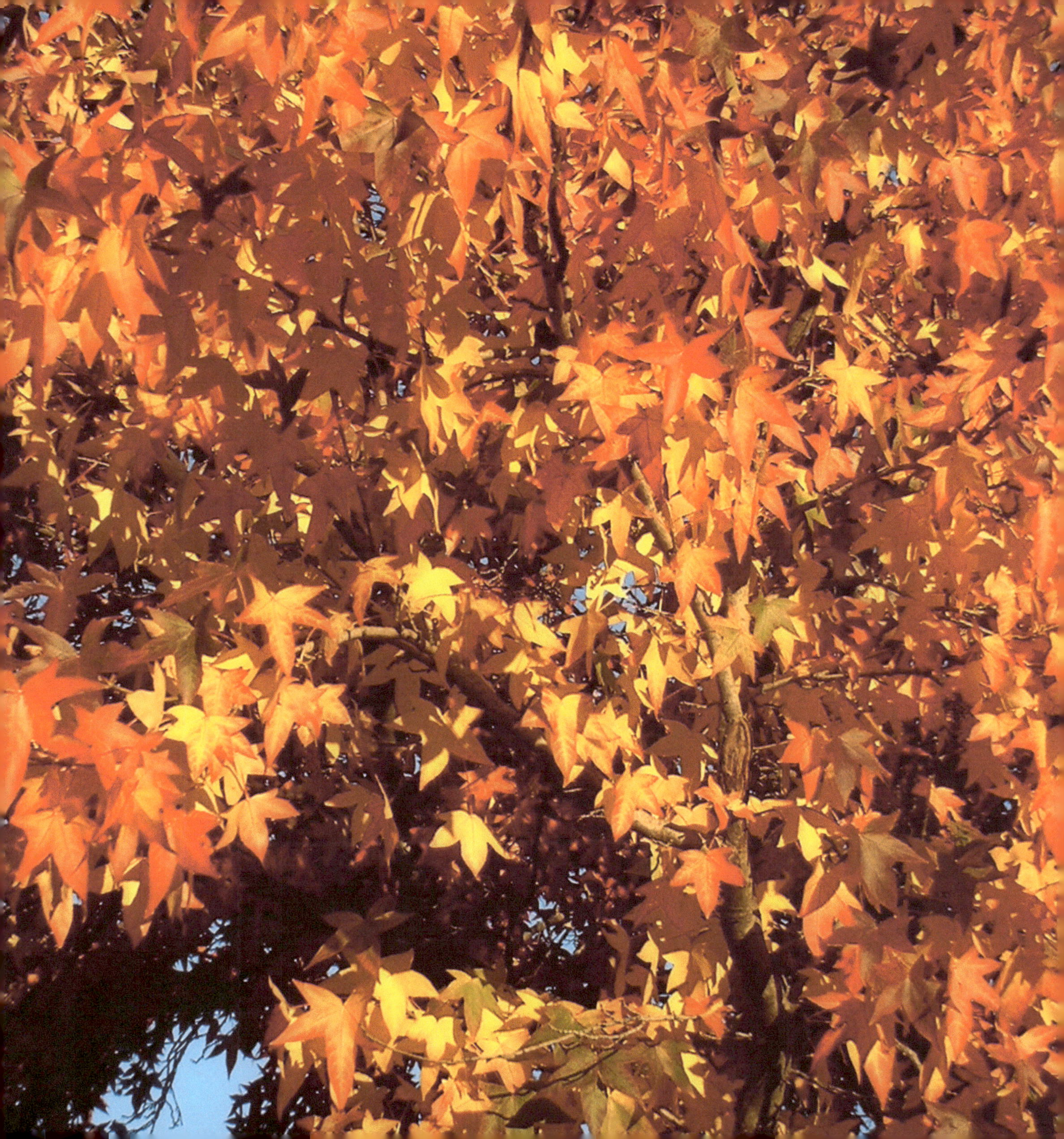

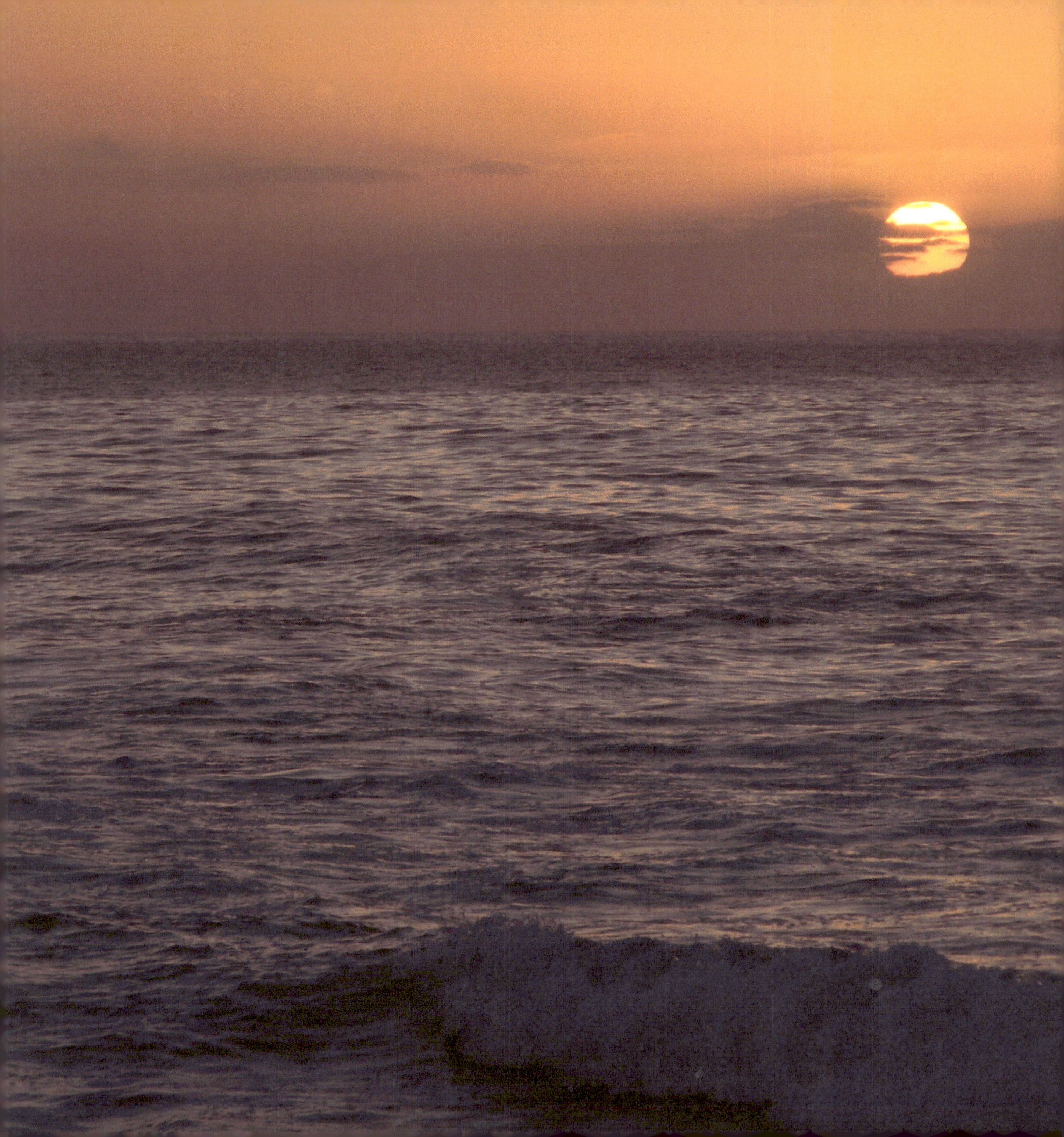

for what is life if in life living and in living death
oh but for what is dying if in dying brings life
oh but woe for thee if in living choose death
for then in dying death bring
but for thee in living choose life in dying life living
for it was unto death that life did come
that in our death we may have life
yet if in living we choose not life
life mayest well have stayed dead
yet life chooseth to die that he might live
and in living life give

‘home’

the beauty of your face, as I sit in this space
your love surrounds me like a well worn glove
you gift me so much peace, so deep an inner release
time with you so sweet, the tears roll as I fall at your feet
kneeling in this space, seeing my reflection in your face
so surreal, so pure, giving myself over to your allure
unguarded and safe, I am home, this is where I belong
I’ve been away far too long
tears blur my sight, but I’m seeing you so clearly
my eyes can be closed but my heart knows
my heart knows this is where I belong
close enough to hear your song
close enough to know you will never depart
close enough to hear your voice in my heart

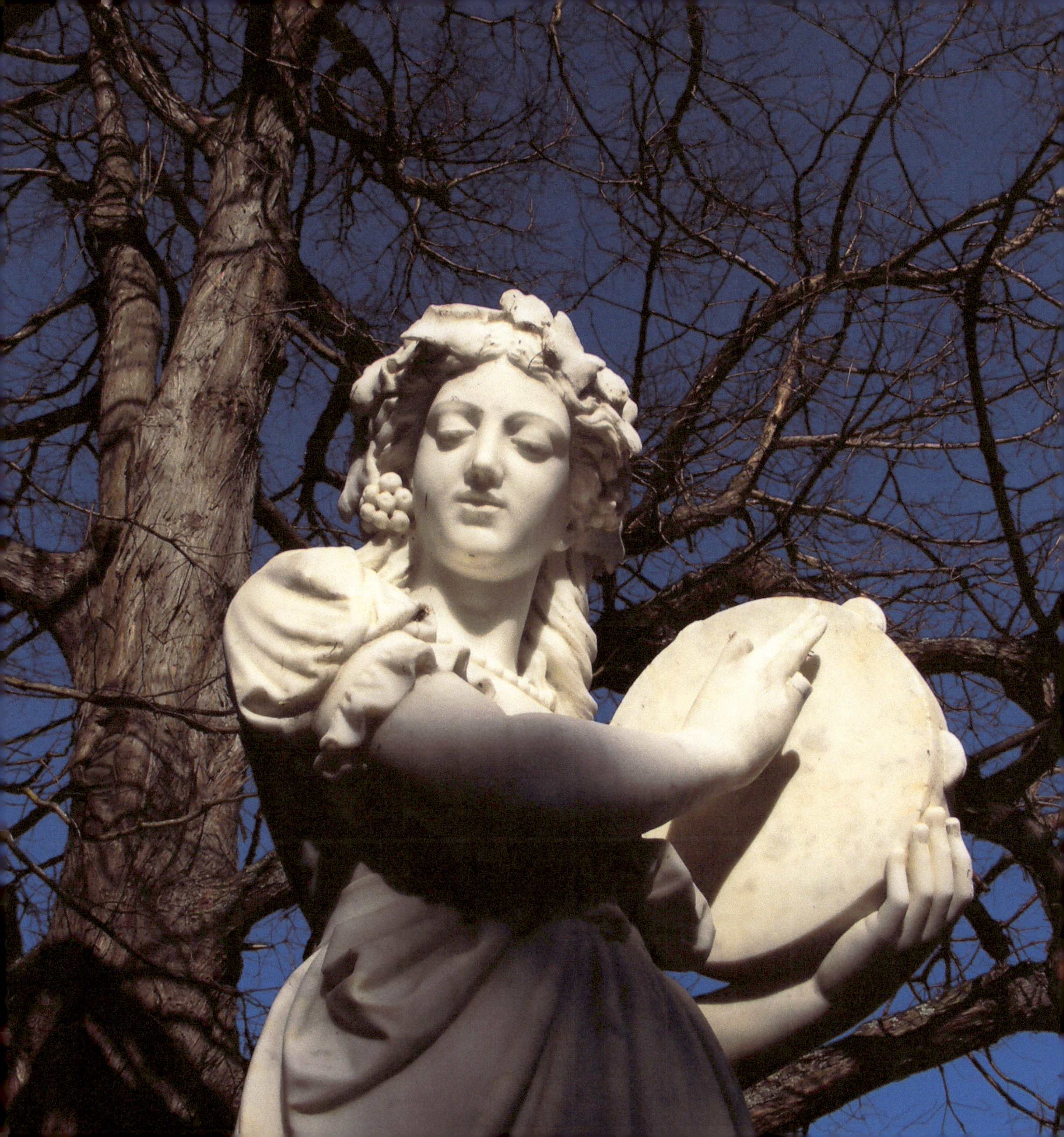

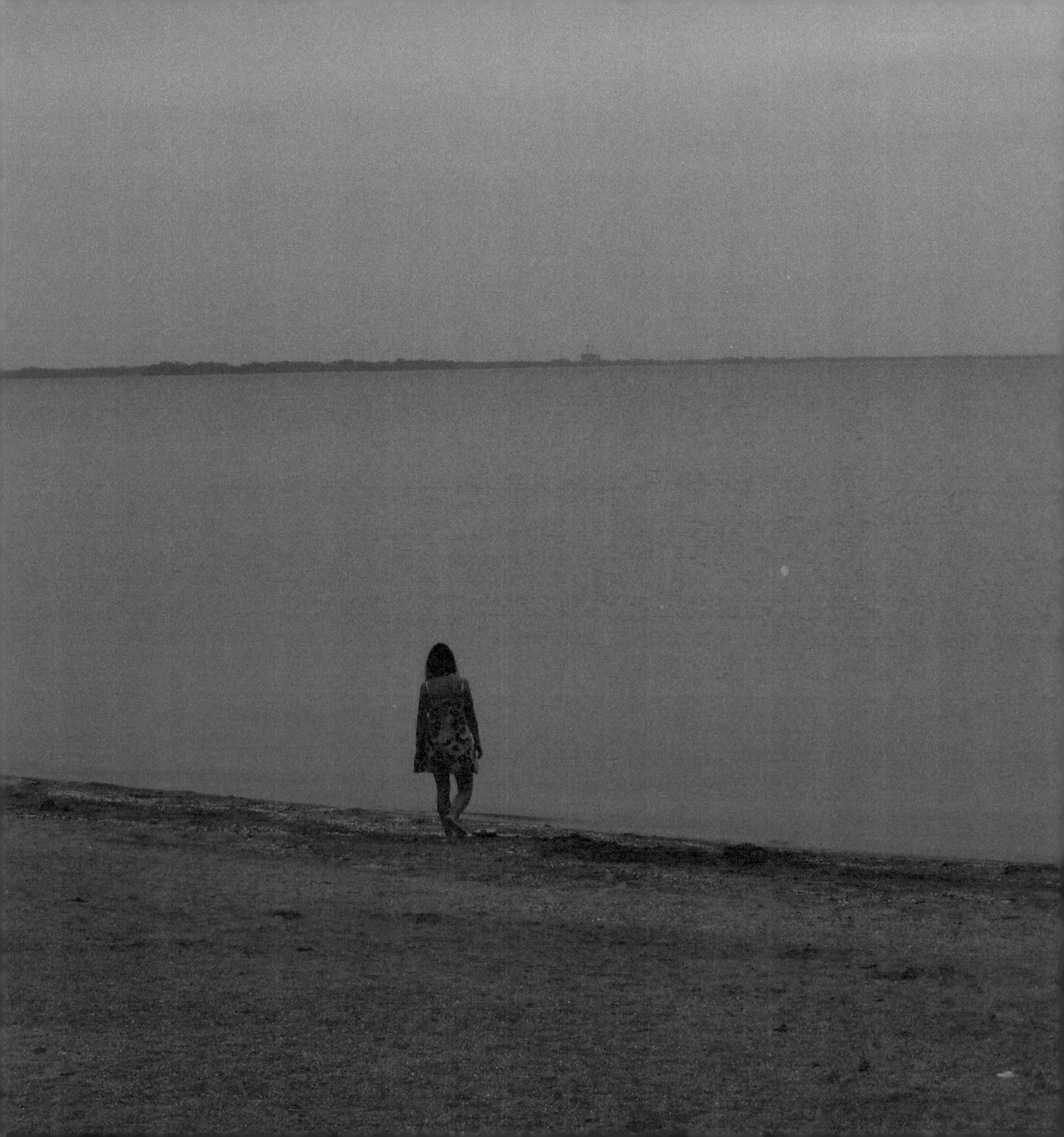

'to the lady of the lake'

I've seen the water cascading over the falls at Niagara
I've heard the wind whistling through the Grand Canyon
but by this one thing I long to abide, I want to be by your side
I've felt the force of the desert sun on my head
I've tasted the salty water of the seven seas
but there's nothing I want more than to be with you on my knees
I've seen the most beautiful birds in the rainforests of Indonesia
I've climbed the tallest buildings in the world
but there's just one thing I wish to do and that's to be with you
I've captured the tears in a child's eyes as he sees his mother dying
I've witnessed the anguish in a mothers face knowing she has run her race
yet I long to see my reflection in your eyes
I long to be that close to feel your lashes touch mine
I've felt the buffalo herd move the earth where I stood
I've cheered as the final runner of the marathon has crossed the line
but of all these thoughts one still remains
and it's you, it is you.

'memories'

she was just a one night stand
the drummer of the local band
I knew picking her up from the bar it wouldn't go far
I just wanted to walk out the door, but she wanted more
she thought I was someone to be found, like a lost dog from the pound
but I had to draw the line in the sand, she was just another one night stand
well that one night stand turned from two, to three, to four
and before I knew it I was no longer waking up and looking out that door
a house, a wife, three kids, my single life had really hit the skids
she was just a one night stand, until I was slipping on that wedding band
now she's making music in my soul, and in her ears are two rocks of coal
as the stars glimmer away, and our bodies continue to sway
there is just one thing I pray, that she will still be here in the new light of day
she was my last one night stand, now she holds my heart in her hand

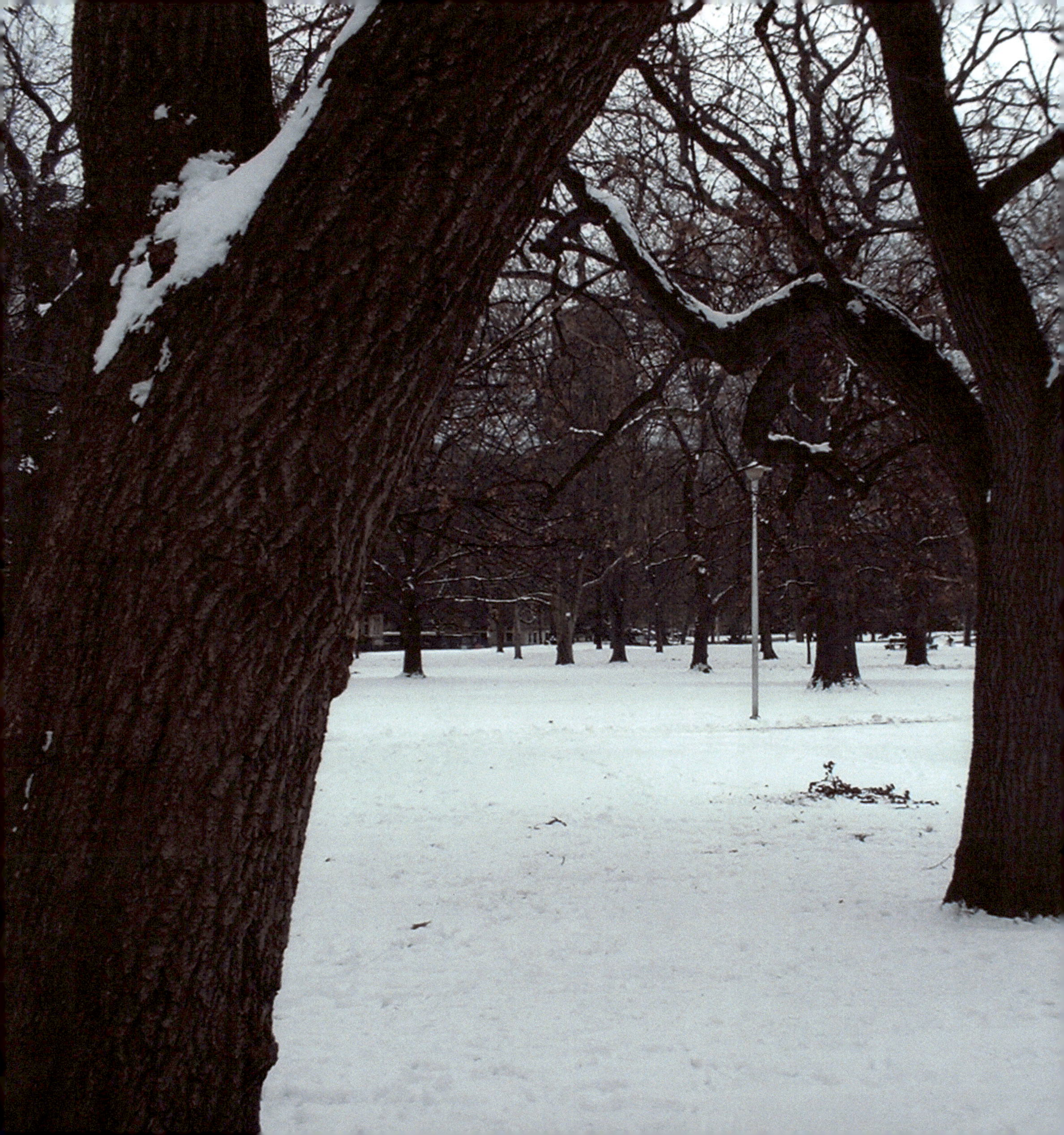

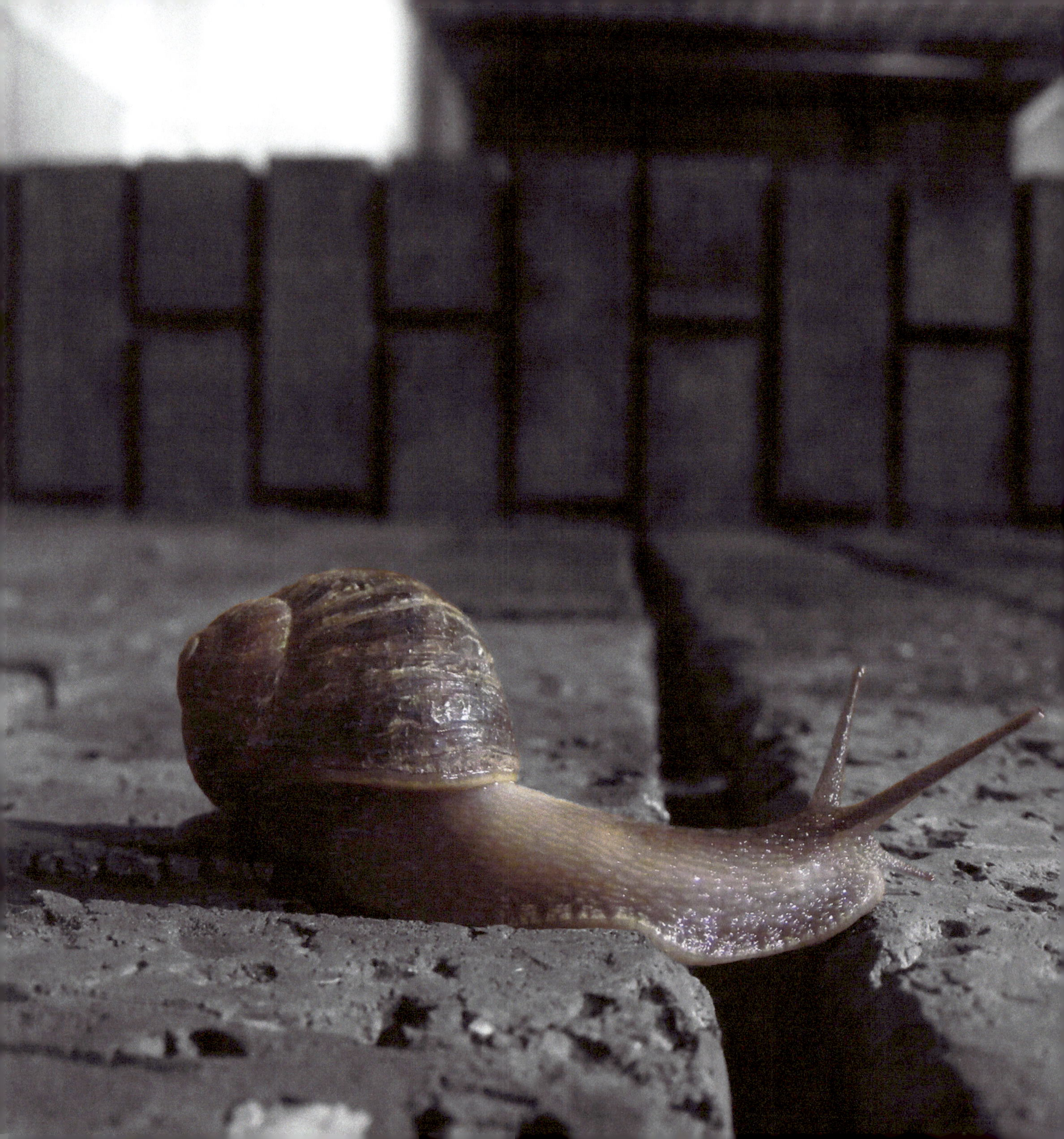

'Mr Snail'

Mr snail, what words do you have to tell
What have you seen as you've travelled the world in your tiny shell
Are they words of wisdom, or a song of prose inspired by your latest rose
Who was your last muse, what does it take to light your fuse
You travel so slow, yet on and on you go
What must I do to make your words flow
All those sights and sounds
What in this life have you found
Have you seen compassion and hope
Have you witnessed those barely able to cope
Have you seen the rich, the poor, and those passed out drunk on the floor
Have you seen the beauty of new life amongst this world of strife
Oh Mr snail what words do you have to tell
What must I do to make you shed your shell
Have you been on a plane to see how other worlds live
Mr snail what wisdom do you have to give
please Mr snail share with me that I might live
please Mr snail.

'route 66'

she sat on the stool , as we spent the night playing pool
her legs covered in black, from the moment I saw her I thought she was whack
singing to tunes on the jukebox, the light shimmering in her luscious locks
guys were buying her drinks all night, asking her if she'd like a light
as the sun chased the moon away, the rumour was spreading that she was gay
last drinks were called and I knew I had to make my move
walking over I was totally in my groove
asking her would she like me to walk her home
when she said yes I was smiling like a garden gnome

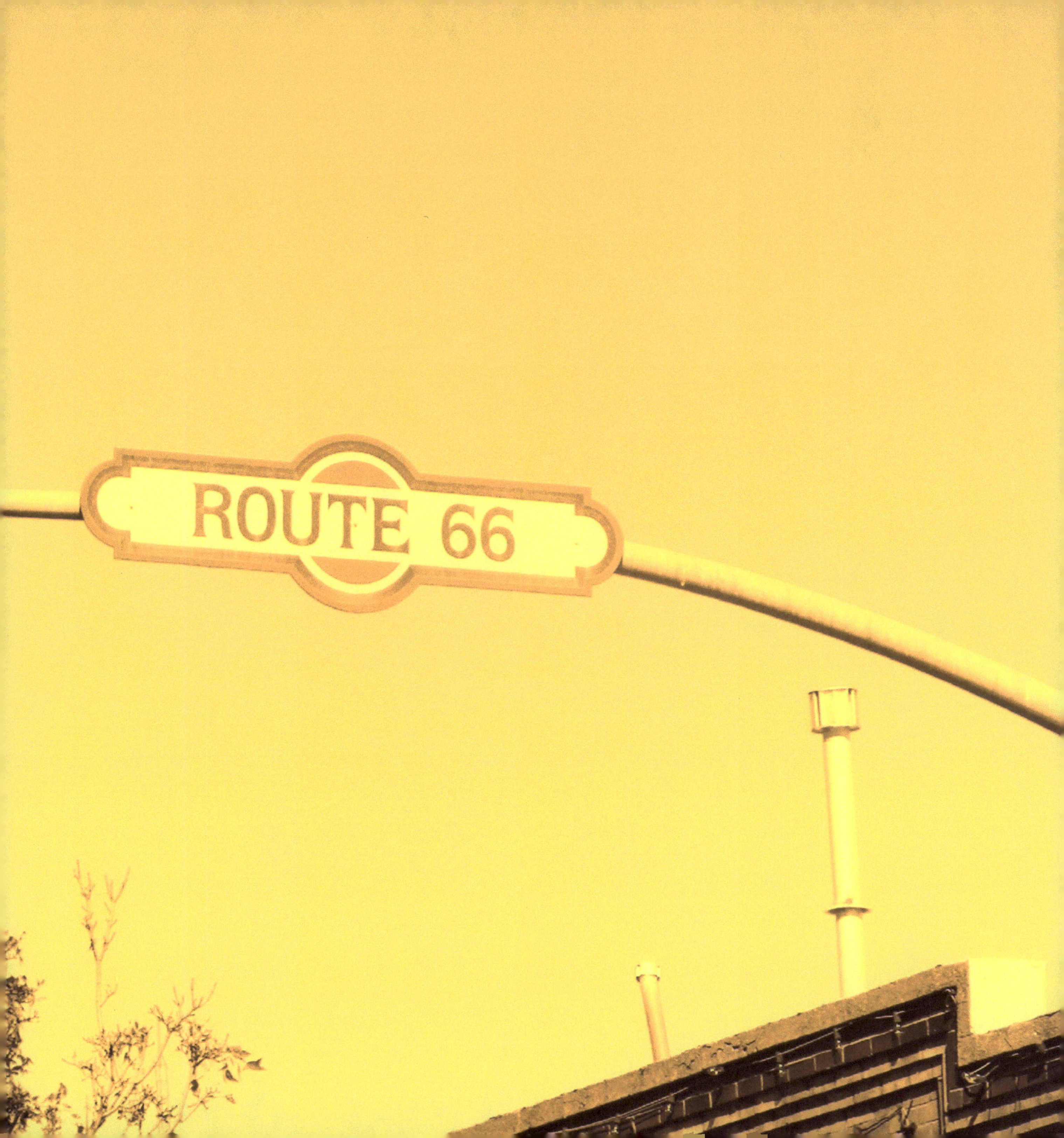

ROUTE 66

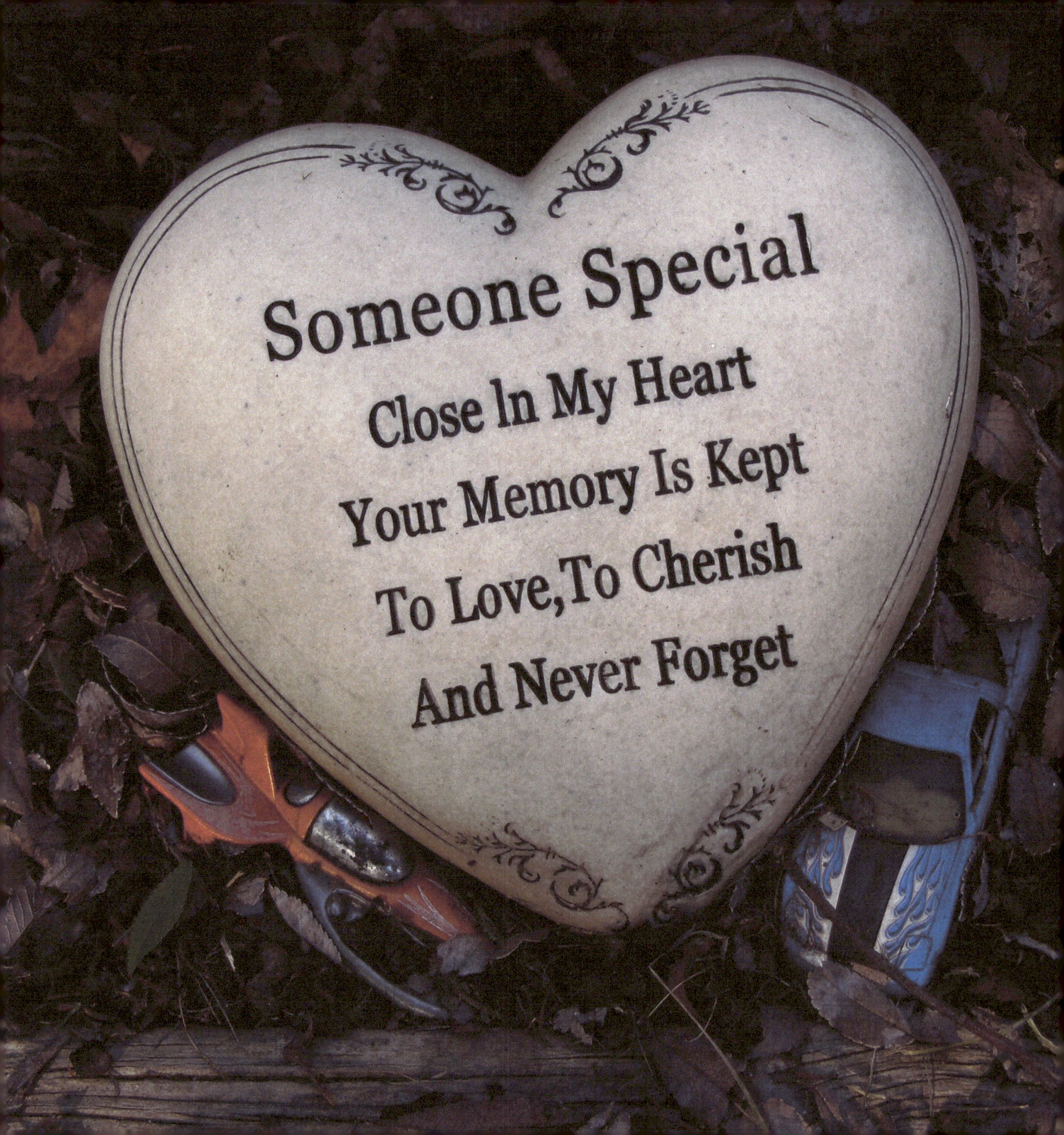
Someone Special
Close In My Heart
Your Memory Is Kept
To Love, To Cherish
And Never Forget

'to the son I never knew'

how do you mourn a son you never knew
how do you count the candles you never blew
how do you know you love a white Christmas when you've never seen the snow
so many memories that were only ever dreams
so many thoughts that will never be shared
I sit surrounded by all these flowers
and say your name aloud but it falls on deaf ears
I never got to hold your hand, or create art works with you in the sand
I never got to teach you how to kick the ball, or watch you get up after your first fall
I sit in this field of flowers and trace your name etched into the rock
and wonder how different my life would have been
would I have lived with your mum, would I have been a great dad
so many questions that will never be answered
you'd be 12 today, yet here you lay
12 years I could have spent calming your fears
12 years I've spent drying my tears
so many memories that were only ever dreams
so many dreams that never got to be memories
love dad.

'pictures of you'

if I die tonight know that you were a light
that kept this fire burning that kept these wheels churning
if I don't see another sunrise know that I died gazing into your eyes
so deep so surreal, constantly enticing me to tell you how I feel
know that you meant the world to me, closing my eyes I could dream of flying free
floating through the clouds, my love for you knows no bounds
oh the pictures you would send to save me from going around the bend
it never mattered of what, though some I liked a little, and some I liked a lot
if I die tonight know that you were the light
that kept this fire burning, that kept these wheels churning
you saw me for all I could be, even when I wanted to flee
you were the voice inside my head, even when you weren't beside me in my bed

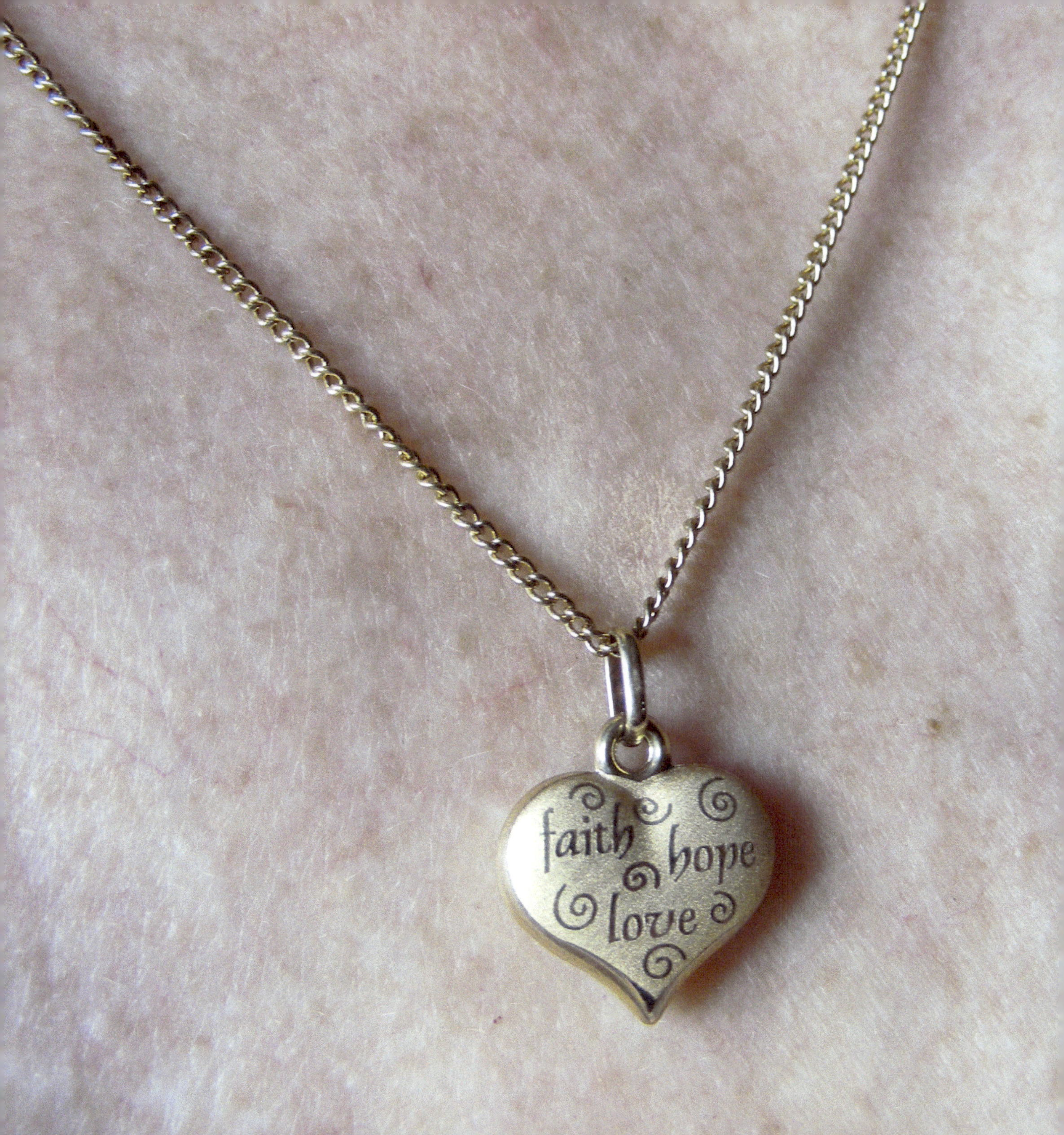
faith
hope
love

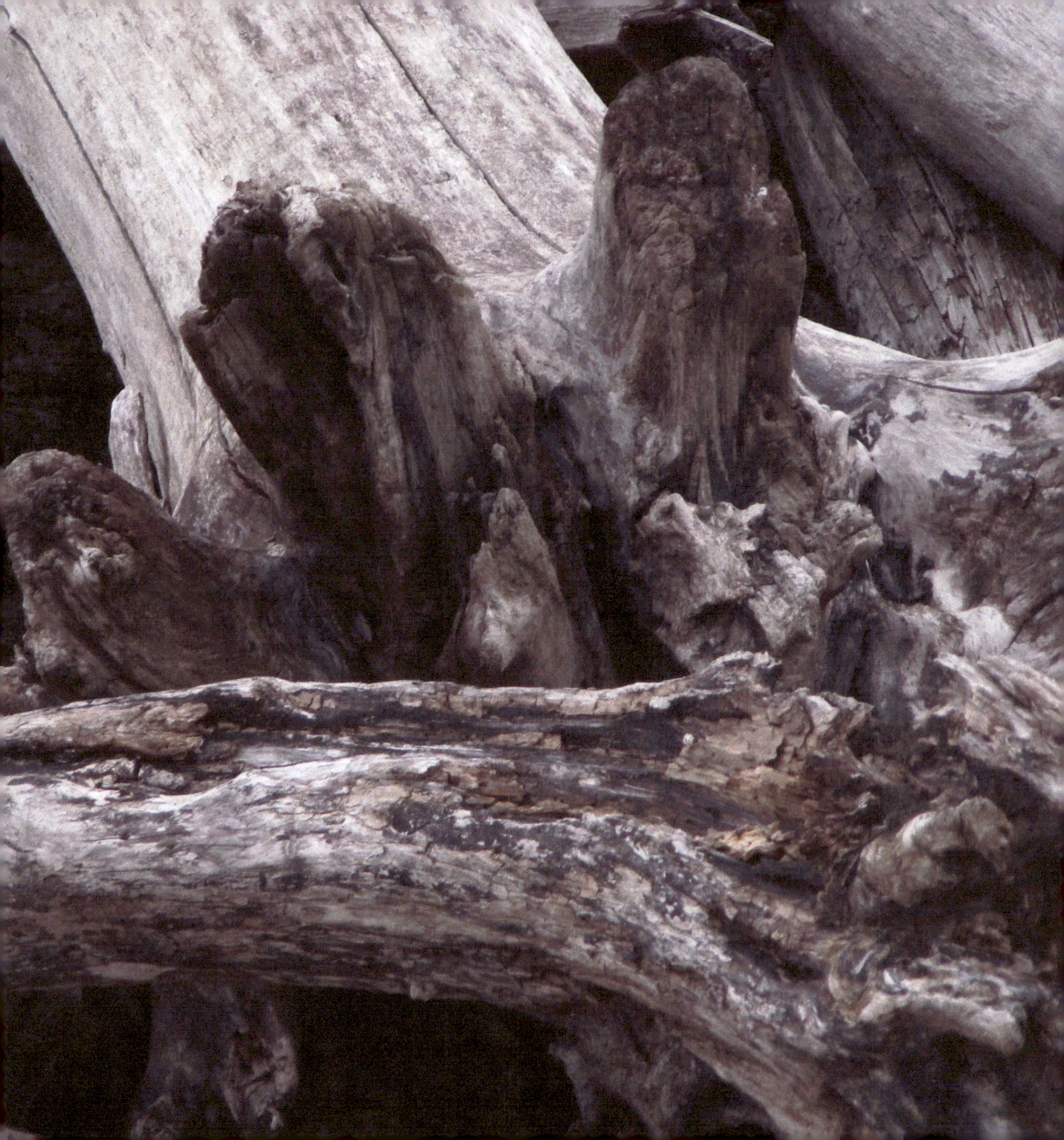

'so this is xmas'

sitting here with bracelets on my wrists
thinking of all the birthdays I would have missed
the sound of the water keeps me awake
as I unscrew the cap and say goodbye to Jake
he was true blue, fair dinkum and all that
now the early morning sun warms the earth where he last sat
a tiny piece of metal the difference between life and death
a tiny piece of metal before his last breath
now the wind carries him away
on this river bank is how I spend my christmas day

it's been a long while since I last knew you
since I could just spend the day floating away
where the hours meld together in your loving embrace
the remembrance of your body against mine
and your lips so supple so divine
the sun hot on our skin , the veil of air between us so thin
your fingers tracing my freshly shaved face
as our bodies entwine in another memorable embrace

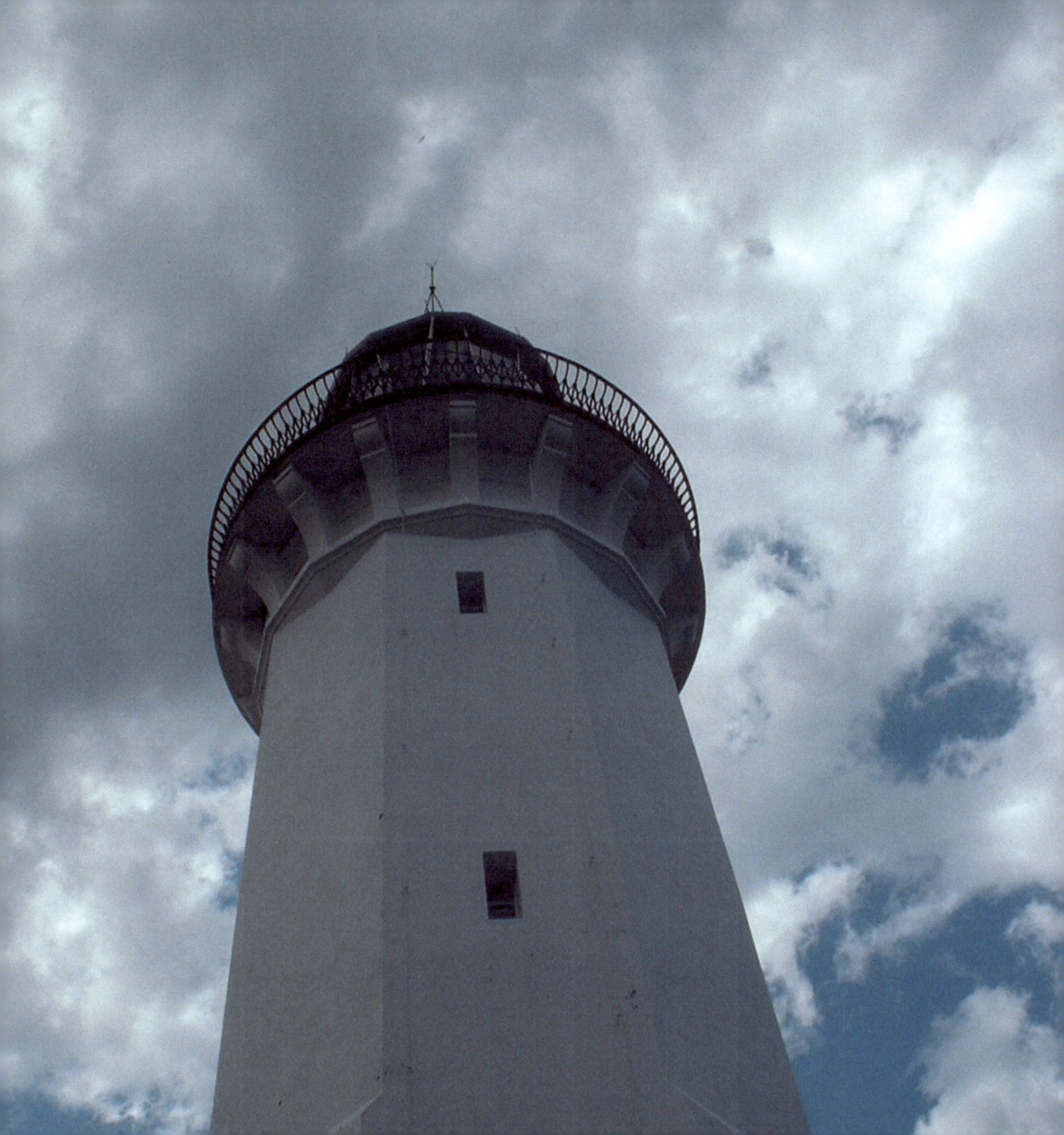

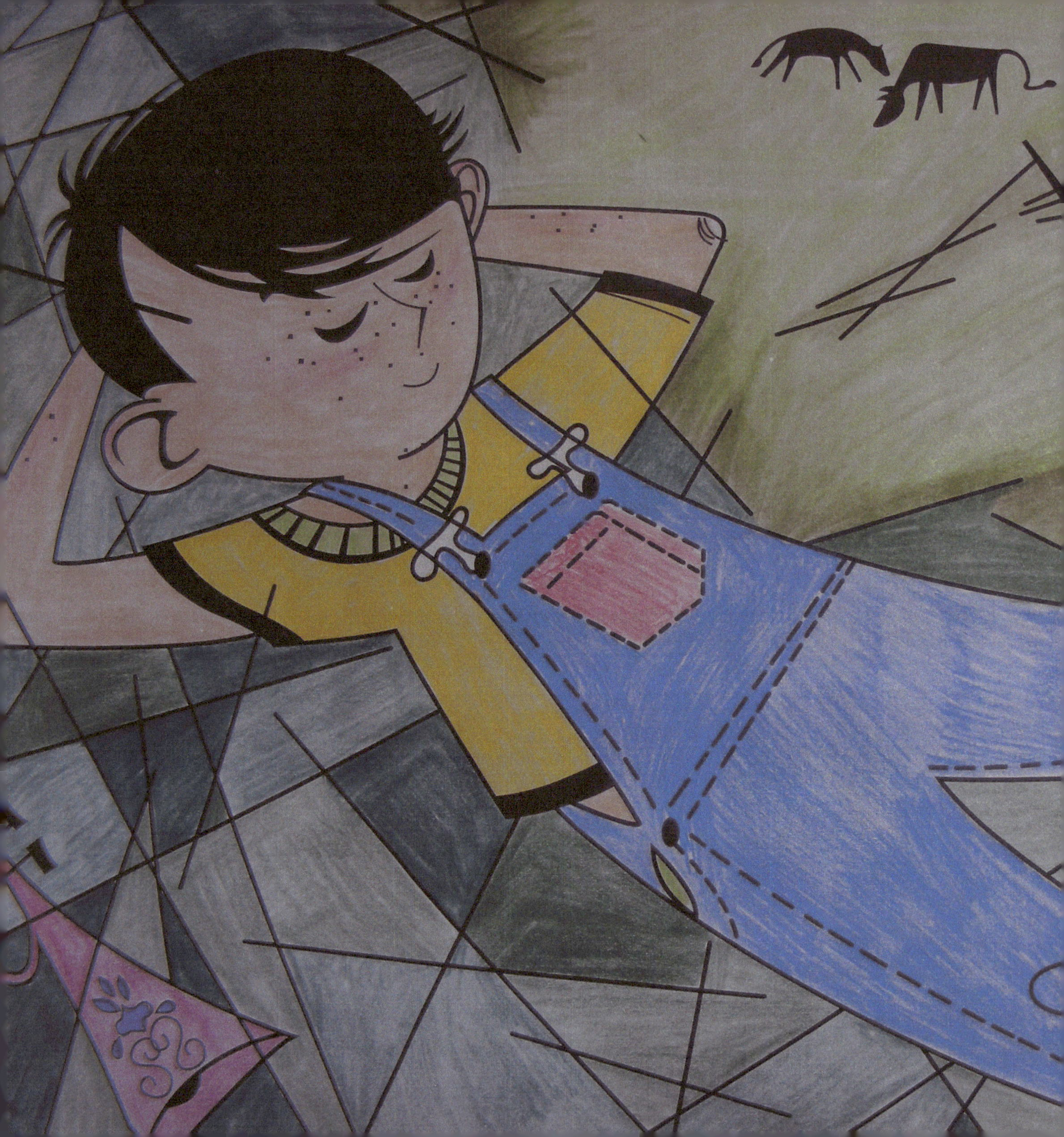

'to my unborn son'

right now you are cells multiplying and dividing at a rapid rate
please know it doesn't matter if you are 18 before your first date
before you are born there's a few things I want you to know
there's a good chance you will really love the snow
if you are anything like me you will feel more than those around you
so be very careful with those that surround you
but most of all know that you are your own self
you might be part of me, and part of your mother, but you are your own self
you will make mistakes and that's okay
though the choices you make live with you till your dying day
you will grow up in a world different to what it is today
but with each day you breathe life, don't waste your time away
you will know heartache and pain, yet you will also taste triumph and gain
when you fall in love you will know the truth in these words
when you see her for the first time you will know
it doesn't matter what your grades are
some of the richest men alive today dropped out of school
yet in all things do your best and follow your heart, it's your strongest tool
when it rains be thankful for the nourishment of the earth
and when it's sunny a tan is not cool
learn from your great grandfather he was a young fool
you will have more opportunities than ever before
but never lose connection with those closest to you
I've said it already but I will say it again
you will know sorrow and pain
but these are but the moderator to happiness and joy
everyone leaves this life at some point, so every chance you get explore the joint
but most of all your name is not your identity
it is simply a word to identify you
you will be known by how you choose to live this life.

'the matrix'

Mozart, Picasso, Leonardo, they all tried to capture your beauty, your grace,
yet here I stand in their place
I cannot paint, I cannot sing but here you lay wearing my diamond ring
those wrinkled lines around your eyes, but a small reminder how quickly time flies
the freckles on your nose even more beautiful than your gorgeous toes
that smile, those lips, as my fingers trace the edge of your hips
leaving kisses on your breast, as I lean my head on them, my heart is at rest
so peaceful, so quiet how did we find this place,
hidden away from the rest of the human race
here amongst the trees and flowers,
becoming even more entrapped by your womanly superpowers
in black and white or colour, with you there is no other
your skin so soft, oh the memory of our first time in your loft
your hair down past your shoulders, that fire in your eyes I see how it smoulders
oh my darling, my sweet, I'm so glad you never let your heart retreat
entrusted with your care, you let me see even more than what I see here, as you lay bare
the sun hot on your skin, I'm so glad each day you let me a little further in
now that we lay here entwined, your heart is my greatest find
I could mine this land till my days were through,
but nothing I could find would be as valuable as you
I could travel this globe and have a girl in every port,
but while you're alive with none other will I consort
your eyes their colour so deep,
every moment I spend in their gaze a bounty so rich I do reap
I'm being silly I know, but when I'm with you I just seem to glow
I know I make you out to be more than you are, but to me you truly are a star
to me you are my little red pill, when I'm with you time truly does stand still

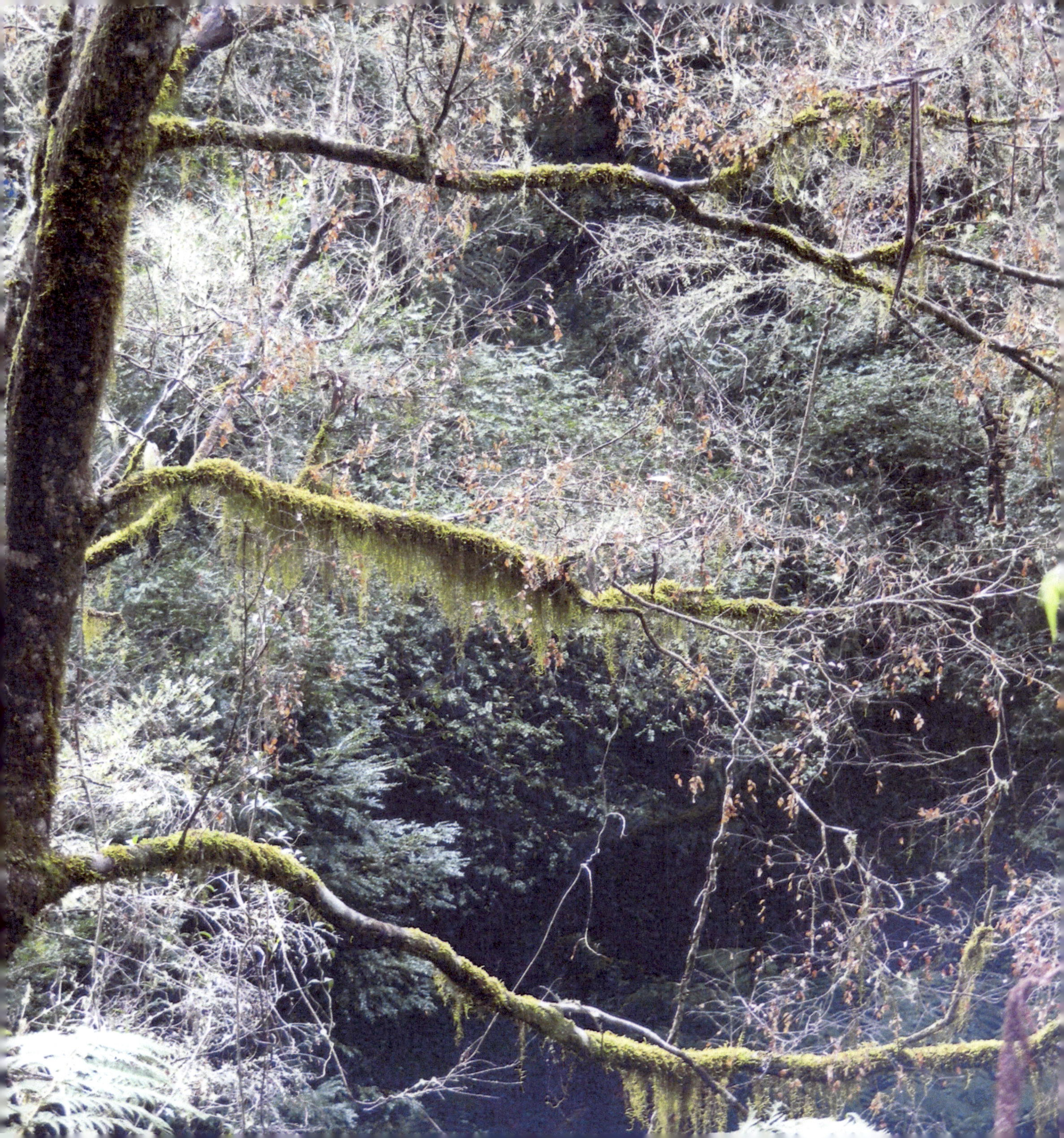

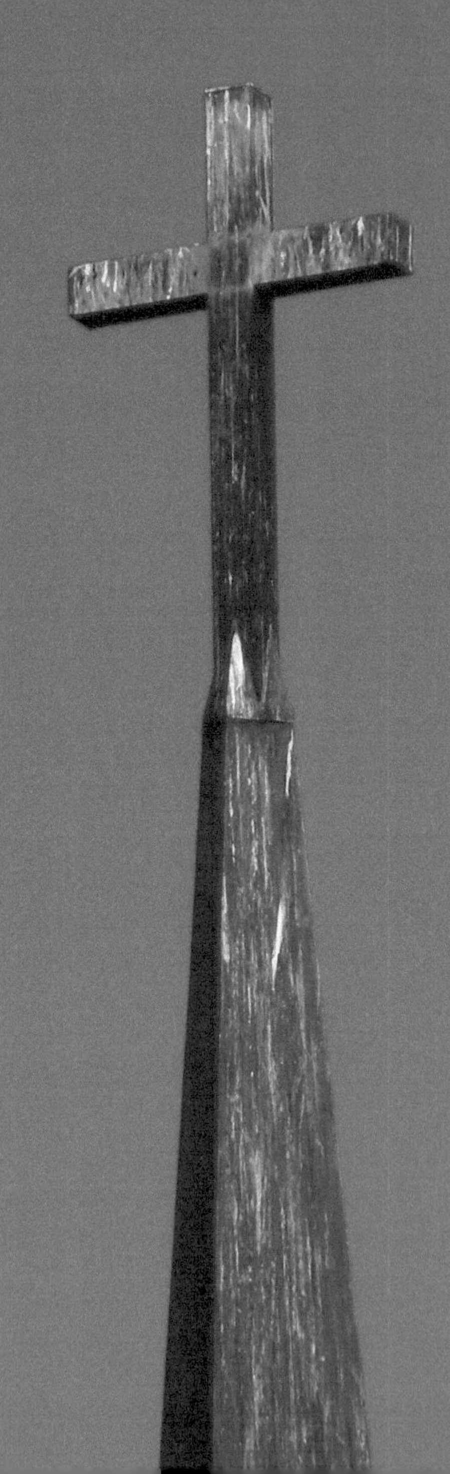

'walking tall'

there he sat in the church pew
so young and naive without a clue
of what was to lay ahead
of who would creep into his bed
but now he is a man
sitting in his lap his biggest fan
the time he spent in between
this poem is but a gleam
a small glimpse of a fortunate life
a succession of years of overcoming strife
as a kid he heard the stories of david, goliath and saul
then reality hit and he had to choose, walk tall, or fall

'dust'

there it sits collecting dust on the shelf
forgotten and neglected
superseded many times over
once a vital part of her life
inseparable until her sweet sixteenth
now its sits surrounded by memories from another life
other things have taken it's place
so many things to do and places to go
she no longer has time for things like that
so many things have changed since then
now she's busy, busy, busy
it once held her every dream in it's heart
now it sits hidden from view collecting dust.

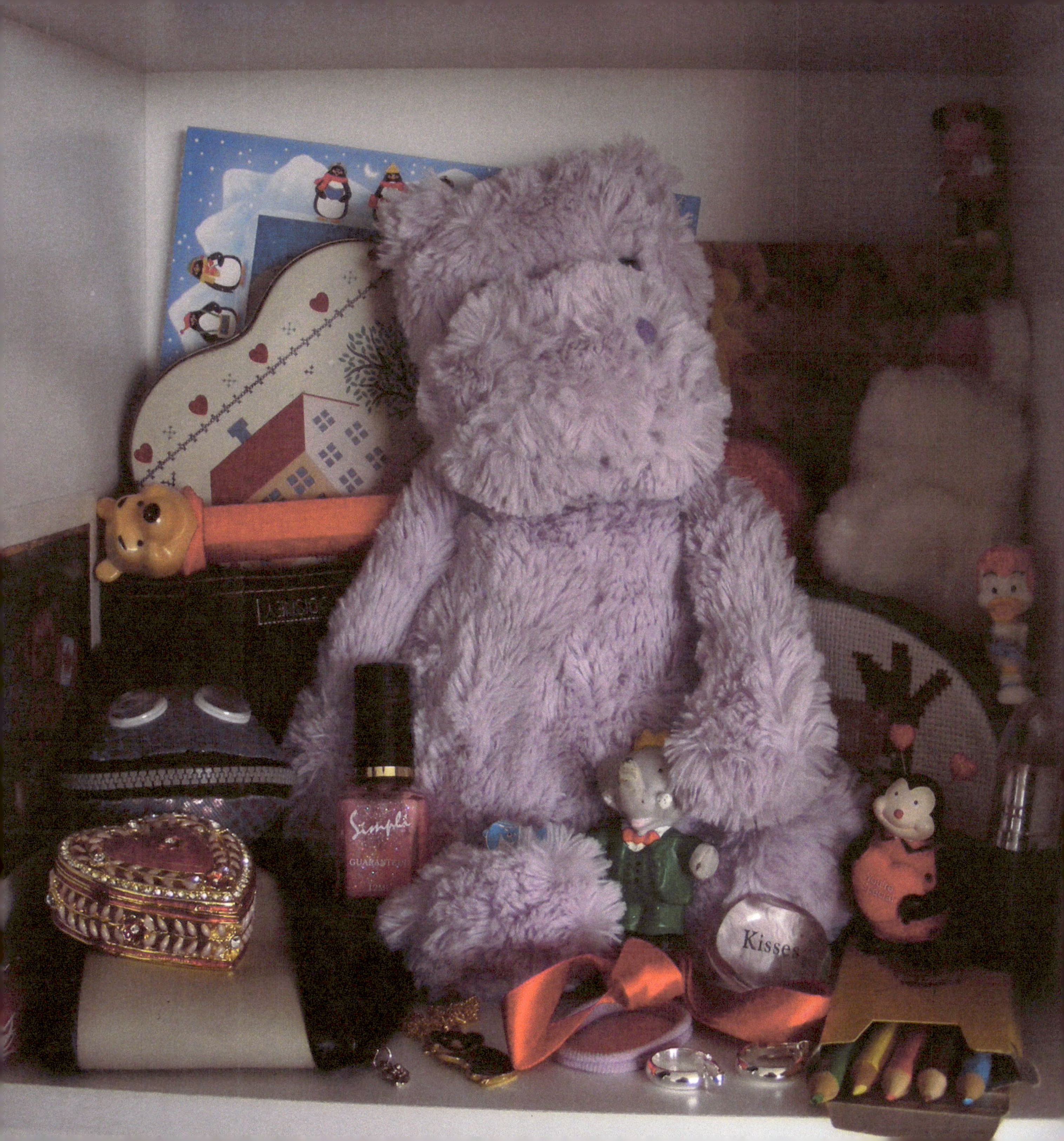
Kisses

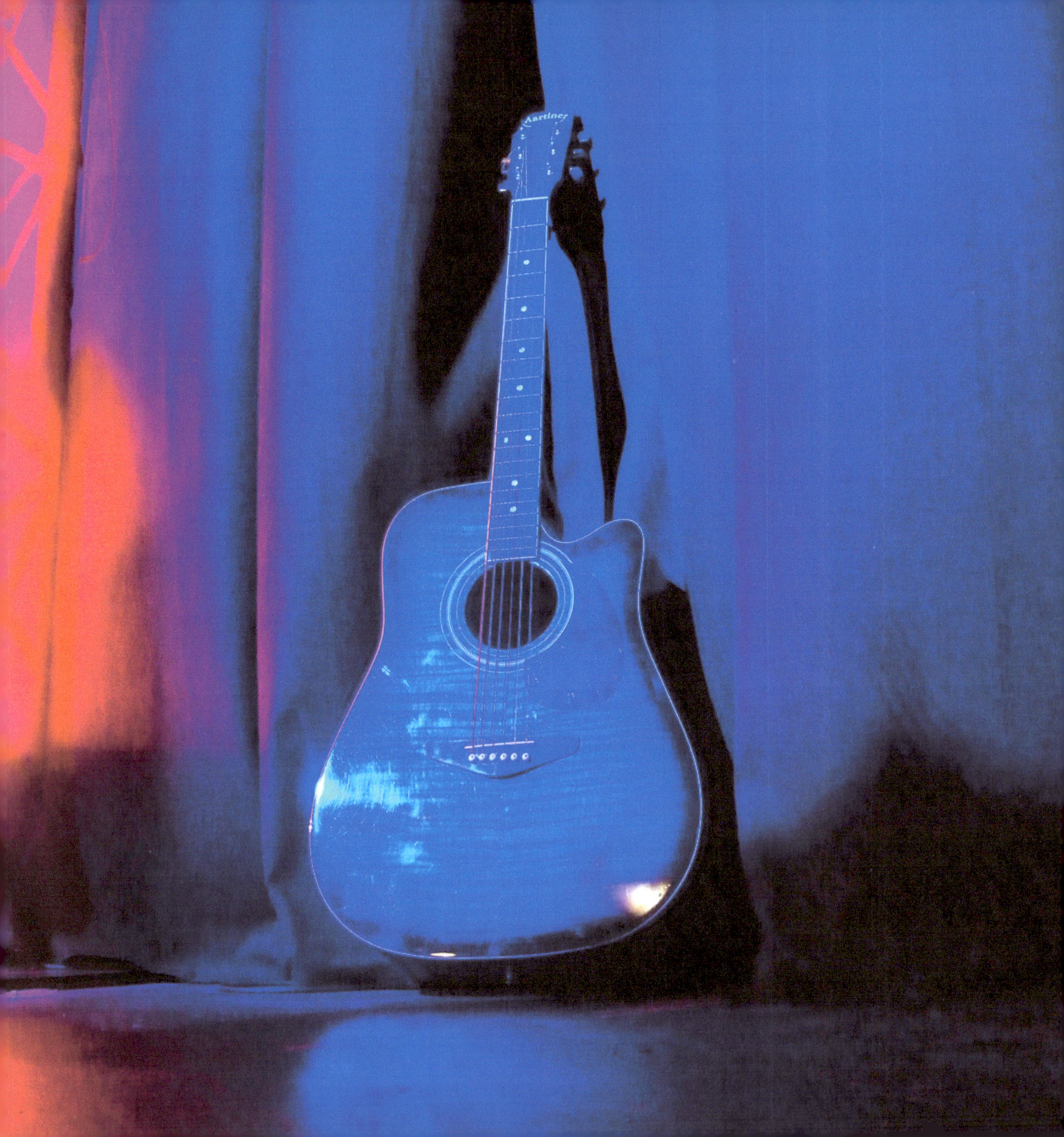

‘tonight’

the lights are dimmed
the fog machines are silent
thousands of eyes have paid to see me
yet they are all looking at you
sitting there in the front row
surrounded by so many strangers
but you don’t see them
all you see is me sitting on the edge of the stage
my guitar in my lap the light shining off the strings
as I sing the first line I see your eyes glass over
a teardrop running down your face
it’s just you and me in this space
I’ve sung the song a hundred times before
but tonight, in this moment, the words,
tonight, it’s you and me
tonight everyone can feel my love for you
tonight.

'if you were my rib'

would I take you to work
or the park
would I fall asleep in front of the tv with you
or read you love sonnets before bed
if you were my rib would I sleep with you in an unmade bed
or make the bed with fresh sheets every night
would I never take a holiday
or fill your passport with stamps every year
if you were my rib would I drink away the overtime
or pour myself into our kids
if you were my rib would you read romance novels longingly
or would we be writing our own best seller together
if you were my rib this poem would never end
if you were my rib

A THOUSAND COUNTRY ROADS
ROBERT JAMES WALLER
timewarner paperbacks

boymeetsgirl
JOSHUA

OLAS SPARKS At First Sight

N CARSON GIFTED HANDS

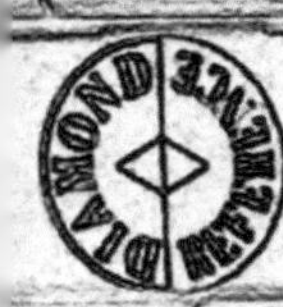

WEDDING PLANNER

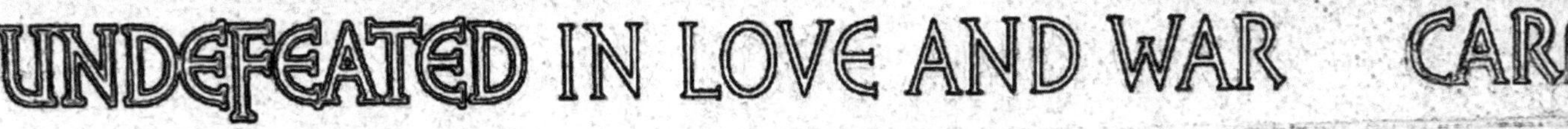

MARS AND Venus IN LOVE JOHN GR

THE LITTLE BOOK OF HUGS Ka

THE PURPOSE DRIVEN® Life WARRE

A. B. FACEY A FORTUNATE LIFE
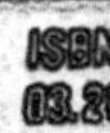

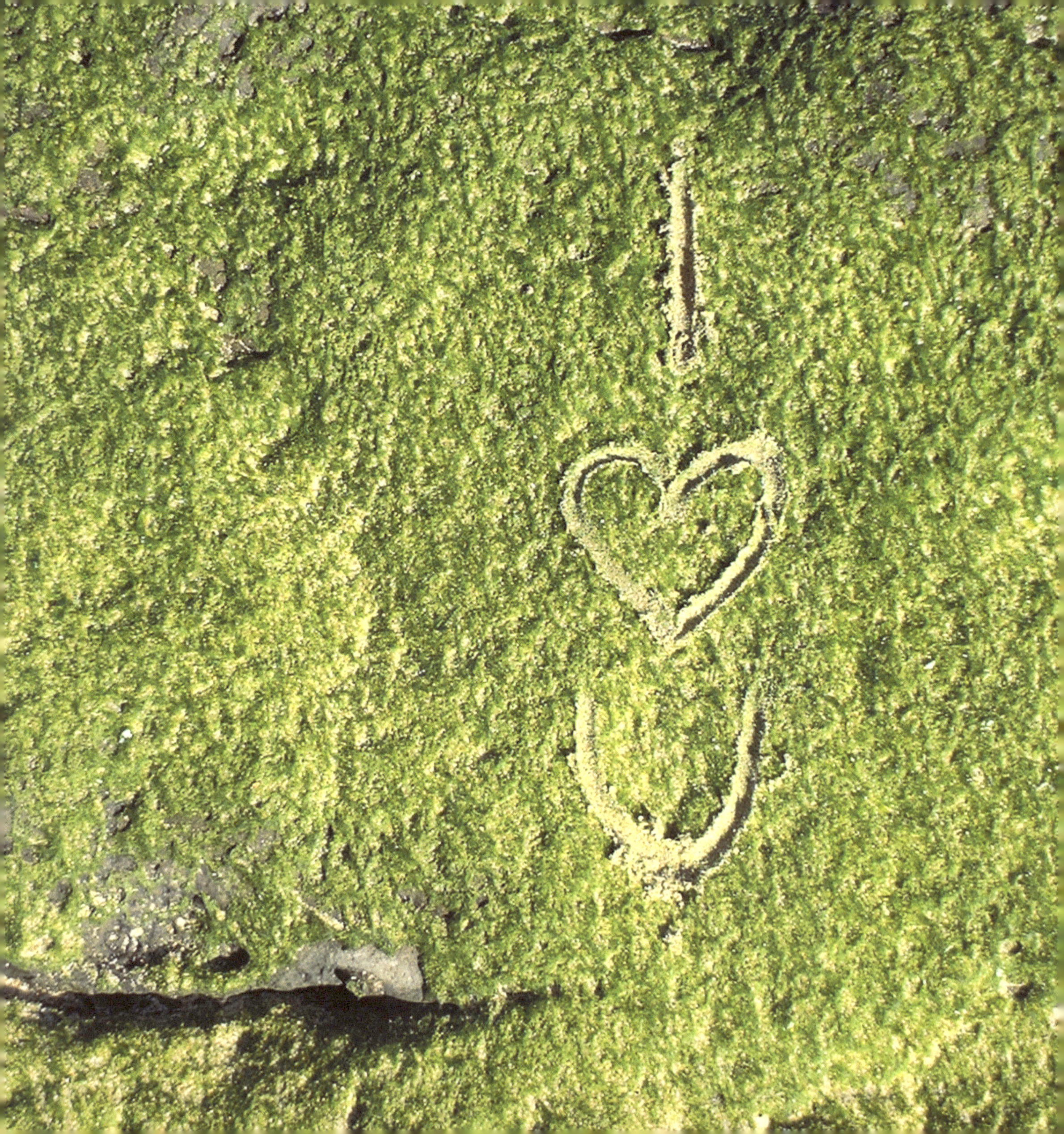
I ♥ U

'muse 2003'

there she sat with a grin on her like a cheshire cat
reading my latest prose, dangling her foot at me covered in hose
perhaps you have a muse she said as if it was more information she did seek
playfully I replied, a muse, I know not of which you speak
with a laugh she volleys back, perhaps a muse that you think is whack
why ma'am it sounds like you think this muse may have broken my fuse
her reply is quick, no, just lit it a few times I presume
oh love, of whom of this wicked crime do you accuse
maybe it is the laughter in me she is trying to exhume
her laughter rings in my ears, a sound I could listen to for years
is she fair and sweet, or devious and wicked with a racing heart beat
is she putting me under a spell and if she was could I tell
weaving a wonderful spell of torments and delights
sending me soaring to many new heights
what is this sweet and wicked muse's name
come now my love I'm only playing a silly foolish game
you know there is no other I would rather kiss
you know it is you I always miss

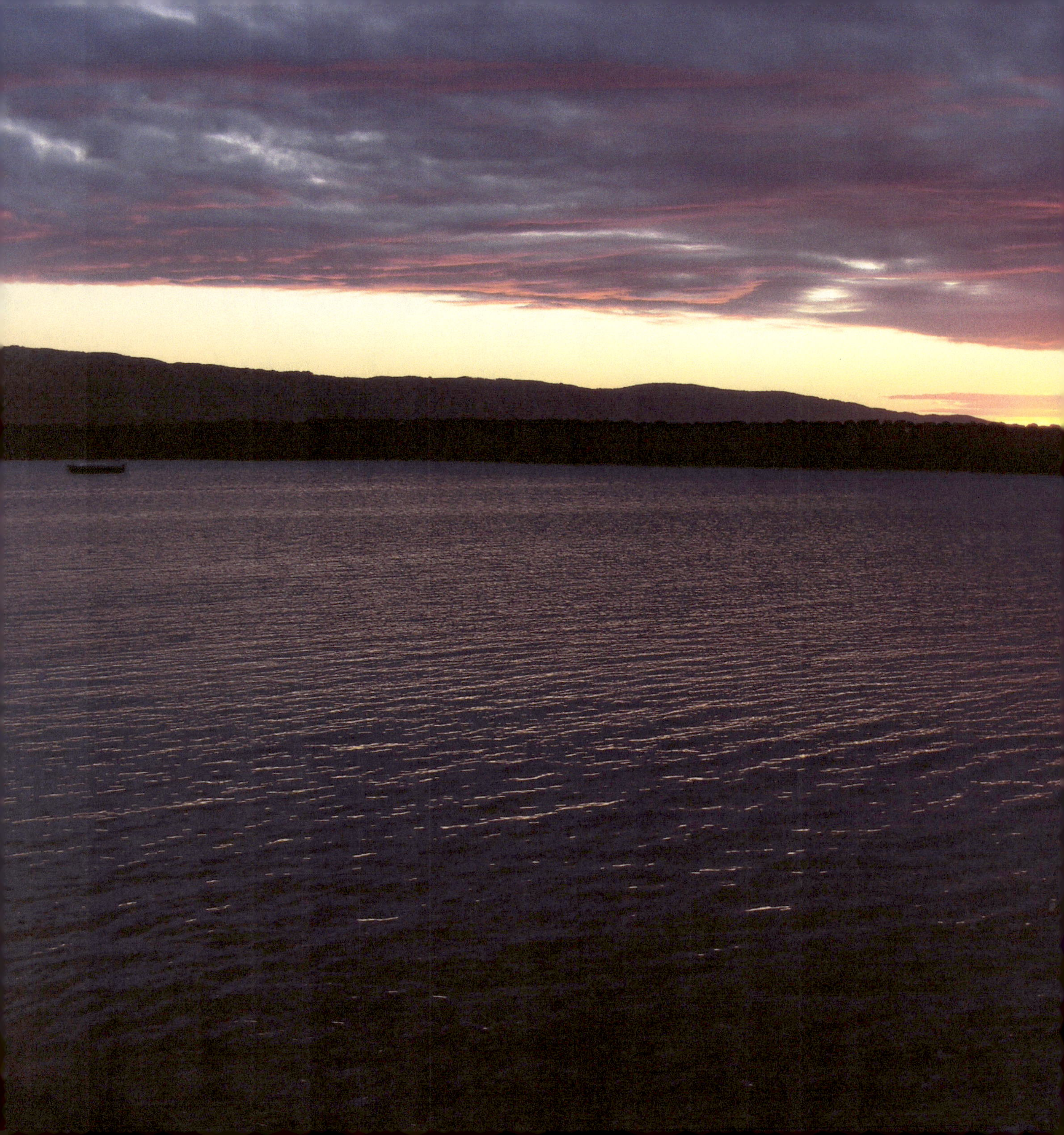

www.ingramcontent.com/pod-product-compliance
Lightning Source LLC
LaVergne TN
LVHW070222110826
845147LV00003B/627

* 9 7 8 0 9 9 2 3 6 1 0 2 0 *